# Tulsidas Ke 50 Dohe

# Tulsidas Ke 50 Dohe

## 50 Lessons For Entrepreneurs

(Connecting Ancient Indian Wisdom
with Entrepreneurship)

(With Hindi Shloka Explained in Hindi and English
and Connecting with Entrepreneurship)

**Prof (Dr) Sanjeev Chaturvedi**

GenNext Publication

*Published by*

GenNext Publication
5, Ansari Road
Daryaganj, New Delhi-110002
Phone: 011-47034999, 9811692060
E-mail: gennextpublication@hotmail.com

*Distribution Network*
gyanbooks.com
India, USA, Canada, UK, Australia, France



ISBN: 978-93-5663-759-7 (PB)
First Published, 2024

*Printed at:* Gyan Press, Delhi.

This book is dedicated to
my mother Late Shrimati
**SHEELA CHATURVEDI**
**(Ammaji)**
and on Opening of
**RAM MANDIR**
**IN AYODHYA IN 2024**

# Acknowledgement

This book is a small effort to connect Indian Wisdom with Modern Entrepreneurship. I must thank first Geeta Press, Gorakhpur, India for providing one of the best books on various subjects since 1923. It has been a great help in writing this book with their diverse publications on Goswami Tulsidas.

Secondly, I would like to thank all my teachers/ professors/ students/friends and family members who supported me in writing my 6th book titled "Kabir Ke 50 Dohe-50 Lessons for Entrepreneurs" which was released in 2023, and got good response from readers. Their positive response encouraged me to write this 7th book on Entrepreneurship and connecting it with Tulsidas. I would also like to thank my critics also who gave me the fire in belly, to prove them wrong, at all stages. This book could not be completed without the support and love of my wife Richa and my two beautiful children Vartika and Vedant.

I am highly obliged to GenNext Publication, New Delhi, who have been constantly supporting me for making my book reachable to a larger section of readers. I must thank the entire team of GenNext Publication for supporting me and in giving final touches and shape to this book.

Finally, I now present this book to all my readers with great humility and modesty, for allowing me to write a book connecting Tulsidas and Entrepreneurship. I am confident that my mistakes will be ignored, and encouragement will be given for making this humble attempt.

**For suggestions, comments, criticism etc.**
**write to me on my personal**
**Email:** sanjeev.chaturvedi2015@gmail.com

# What is Book All About

Rambola Dubey or Tulsidas was born in Rajpur, in the district of Banda in Uttar Pradesh, in Samvat 1589 or 1532 A.D. He was a Sarayuparina Brahmin by birth and is regarded as an incarnation of Valmiki, the author of Ramayana written in Sanskrit. His father's name was Atmaram Shukla Dube and his mother's name Hulsi. It is said, Tulsidas did not cry at the time of his birth. He was born with all the thirty-two teeth intact. In childhood his name was Tulsiram or Ram Bola.

Tulsidas's wife's name was Buddhimati (Ratnavali). Tulsidas's son's name was Tarak. Tulsidas was passionately attached to his wife. He could not bear even a day's separation from her. One day his wife went to her father's house without informing her husband. Tulsidas stealthily went to see her at night at his father-in-law's house. This produced a sense of shame in Buddhimati. She said to Tulsidas, "My body is just a network of flesh and bones. If you would develop for Lord Rama even half the love that you have for my filthy body, you would certainly cross the ocean of Samsara and attain immortality and eternal bliss". These words pierced the heart of Tulsidas like an arrow. He did not stay there even for a moment. He abandoned home and became an ascetic. He spent fourteen years in visiting the various sacred places of pilgrimage.

According to another story, while returning from answering the calls of nature, Tulsidas used to throw the water that was left in his water-pot at the roots of a tree which a spirit was occupying. The spirit was very much pleased with Tulsidas. The spirit said, "O man! Get a boon from me". Tulsidas replied, "Let me have Darshan of Lord Rama". The spirit said, "Go to the Hanuman temple. There Hanuman comes in the guise of a leper to hear the *Ramayana* as the first hearer and leaves the place last of all. Get hold of him. He will help you". Accordingly, Tulsidas met Hanuman, and through His grace, had Darshan or vision of Lord Rama.

Tulsidas wrote twelve books. The most famous book is his Ramayana–*Ram-Charit-manas*–in Hindi. He wrote this book under the directions of Hanuman. This Ramayana is read and worshipped with great reverence in every Hindu homes. It is an inspiring book. It contains sweet couplets in beautiful rhyme. *Vinaya Patrika* is another important book written by Tulsidas.

As per one of the famous tales, some thieves came to Tulsidas's Ashram to take away his goods. They saw a blue-complexioned guard, with bow and arrow in his hands, keeping watch at the gate. Wherever they moved, the guard followed them. They were frightened. In the morning, they asked Tulsidas, "O venerable saint! We saw a young guard with bow and arrow in his hands at the gate of your residence. Who is this man?" Tulsidas remained silent and wept. He came to know that Lord Rama Himself had been taking the trouble to protect his goods. He at once distributed all his wealth among the poor.

Tulsidas lived in Ayodhya for some time. Then he shifted to Varanasi. One day a murderer came and cried, "For the love of Rama give me alms. I am a murderer". Tulsi called him to his house, gave him sacred food which had been offered to the Lord and declared that the murderer was purified. The Brahmins of Varanasi reproached Tulsidas and said, "How can the sin of a murderer be absolved? How could you eat with him? If the sacred bull of Siva–Nandi–would eat from the hands of the murderer, then only we would accept that he had been purified". Then the murderer was taken to the temple and the bull ate from his hands. The Brahmins were put to shame.

Tulsidas once went to Brindavan. He visited a temple. He saw the image of Lord Krishna. He said, "How shall I describe Thy beauty, O Lord! But Tulsi will bow his head only when You take up bow and arrow in Your hands". The Lord revealed Himself before Tulsidas in the form of Lord Rama with bow and arrows.

Tulsidas's blessings brought the dead husband of a poor woman back to life. The Moghul emperor at Delhi came to know of the great miracle done by Tulsidas. He sent Message for Tulsidas. Tulsidas came to the emperor's court. The emperor asked the saint to perform some miracle. Tulsidas replied, "I have no superhuman power. I know only the name of Rama". The emperor put Tulsi in prison and said, "I will release you only if you show me a miracle". Tulsi then prayed to Hanuman. Countless bands of powerful monkeys entered the royal court. The emperor got frightened and said, “O saint, forgive me. I know your greatness now”. He at once released Tulsi from prison.

Tulsi left his mortal coil and entered the Abode of Immortality and Eternal Bliss in 1623 A.D. at the age of ninety-one at Asighat in Varanasi.

# 1

तुलसी साथी विपत्ति के, विद्या विनय विवेक।
साहस सुकृति सुसत्यव्रत, राम भरोसे एक।।

**भावार्थ:**- तुलसीदासजी इस दोहे में कहते हैं कि यदि किसी व्यक्ति में विद्या, विनय, विवेक, साहस, सदाचार, सत्यवादी और भगवान् पर पूर्ण निष्ठा हो तो उसके जीवन की बड़े से बड़ा संकट और जीवन की विपत्तियाँ स्वयं टल जाएंगी।

## Meaning in English

Tulsidas explains here that if any person has Knowledge, Modesty, Wisdom, Fearlessness, Good Mannerism, Honesty and Full Faith in Almighty: Many difficulties and hurdles will automatically disappear.

## Lesson For Entrepreneurs

From this couplet we can say that any entrepreneur who has knowledge, modesty, wisdom, fearlessness, is dignified, honest and have full faith in God, he can never be unsuccessful. Times may be good or bad in his venture, but he will overcome all obstacles of business and come out with a successful and profitable enterprise.

# 2

सूर समर करनी करहिं, कहि न जनावहिं आपु।
बिद्यमान रन पाइ रिपु, कायर कथहिं प्रतापु।।

**भावार्थः**- तुलसी दास जी इस दोहे में कहते हैं कि अच्छा व्यक्ति अपना कार्य करता है बिना किसी को दिखावा किये हुए। ठीक उस योद्धा की भांति जो युद्ध के मैदान में अपना पराक्रम दिखाता है, न कि अपनी वीरता के स्वयं बखान करता फिरता है।

## Meaning in English

Here Tulsidas says that Noble person just continue doing good work what he is supposed to do. He does not talk about it to everyone. Same is with Great Warriors. They don't keep telling stories of their successful war which he has won or his warriorship; but they just go to battle to fight with great courage and fearlessness and come out victorious.

## Lesson For Entrepreneurs

A good entrepreneur does not boast about his product or services which he is offering to market. Instead, he explains the benefits of the product or services to the consumer. He wants that Consumer must talk about his product benefits in the market. He wants that customer should be satisfied and if that is the case, product is automatically successful. Entrepreneur should be confident of his product/service, success will come to him sooner or later.

# 3

आवत ही हरषै नहीं, नैनन नहीं सनेह।
तुलसी तहां न जाइये, कंचन बरसे मेह।।

**भावार्थः**- यदि आपके आने की खुशी सभा में नहीं है और लोगो की दृष्टि में आपके लिए स्नेह नहीं है तो ऐसी जगह पर नहीं जाना चाहिए चाहे वो सभा कितनी ही महत्वपूर्ण क्यों न हो।

## Meaning in English

Here Tulsidas explains that one should not go to place or ceremonies where he is not liked and feel uninvited. He must avoid those places or meeting. These occasion can be very important for him, but he must avoid it at all cost, if he feels that there is no respect or courtesy for him.

## Lesson For Entrepreneurs

Here we can connect this couplet with the entrepreneurs who are not welcomed or given help, by the people/company which he expects them to give business. Even if some company is ready to give business but the people are rude and have no respect for the entrepreneur, he must avoid such business deals at all costs. No business is bigger than respect and right treatment. Hence entrepreneur should always go to places/companies etc which treat him well and help him in whatever way they can. It is more important to have relations with them rather than dealing with wrong people.

# 4

तुलसी मीठे बचन ते, सुख उपजत चहुं ओर।
बसीकरन इक मंत्र है, परिहरू बचन कठोर।।

**भावार्थः**- इस दोहे में मीठी वाणी का गुणगान करते हुए गोस्वामी तुलसीदासजी कहते हैं कि आपके मीठे बोल वातावरण को सुख प्रदान करते हैं। आपकी मीठी वाणी किसी कठोर वचन की तुलना में किसी वशीकरण मंत्र सा प्रभाव सुनने वाले पर डालती है।

## Meaning in English

Tulsidas here tries to explain that speaking correctly and politely bring joy and happiness to people who listen it. On the other hand if you speak harshly, it will bring adverse results from the person. Hence one should speak only good words as it creates magic in the environment.

## Lesson For Entrepreneurs

It is similarly important for Entrepreneurs to speak correctly, accurately and with courtesy/ respect. The listener will have good attention when the other person talks politely. This other person can be your customer, stake holders, partners, employees etc. Everyone wants to listen good and polite words. The chances of getting good results when we speak correctly and politely are immense. It brings lot of benefits and profits to the company and its growth, in the long run.

# 5

तुलसी भरोसे राम के, निर्भय हो के सोए।
अनहोनी होनी नही, होनी हो सो होए।।

**भावार्थः**- तुलसीजी कहते हैं कि स्वयं को ईश्वर के भरोसे रखे और जीवन को पूरी निर्भयता के साथ जिए। यदि आपका कर्म सही है और आपकी ईश्वर के प्रति पूर्ण श्रद्धा भाव है तो किसी प्रकार की अनहोनी नहीं होगी और यदि कुछ अनिष्ट होना है तो परमपिता की कृपा से वो हो कर ही रहेगा इसलिए बेकार की चिंता में जीवन व्यर्थ न करे।

## Meaning in English

Here Tulsidas says that One should have full faith in Almighty and sleep well in night as nothing will happen. God will take care of everything. When Almighty your caretaker, he will protect you from everything bad. Even if sometime bad happens it will also be taken care by God. So, we should stop worrying and sleep well.

## Lesson For Entrepreneurs

Entrepreneurs always go through the stages of Anxiety and Depressions if their business is not going well. As per the couplet above of Tulsidas, Entrepreneurs should not worry about these phases of business. It's a normal business cycles/life. Lossing your sleep over this is extremely unnecessary. Thinking is Good but Worrying is Bad. Hence whenever there is a problem, we must think of finding a solution and stop worrying about it. It's of no use and nothing concrete comes out from being worried. Hence have faith and continue doing your work and Stop Worrying.

# 6

राम नाम मनिदीप धरु, जीह देहरीं द्वार।
तुलसी भीतर बाहेरहुँ, जौं चाहसि उजिआर।।

**भावार्थः**- यदि आप अपने जीवन में ईश्वर का प्रकाश चाहते हैं तो अपने मुख में भगवान् राम का नाम सदैव रखें जैसे घर के द्वार पर रखा दीपक घर के भीतर और बाहर दोनों ओर प्रकाश फैलाता है ठीक उसी प्रकार ईश्वर का नाम आपके मुख से आपके भीतर और बाहर दोनों ओर ईश्वरीय प्रकाश वितरित करेगा।

## Meaning in English

Here Tulsidas explains that if you want True Light in your life keep repeating word "Ram" again and again. As a small earthen lamp if put on the Door, it gives light to both Inside and Outside of the house. Similarly, if you keep repeating name of God Ram, it will enlightened you both from Inside and Outside.

## Lesson For Entrepreneurs

Here we can derive from this couplet is that - Entrepreneur should keep them enlightened with being knowledgeable about their business. Anything happening outside in the market related to their business must be known and secondly you also must understand what is happening within the organisation. Must be aware and adopt to both internal and external environment. Then only you can survive in business and bring happiness to various stake holders.

# 7

सहज सुहृद गुर स्वामी सीख, जो न करइ सिर मानि।
सो पछिताइ अघाइ उर, अवसि होइ हित हानि।।

**भावार्थः**- अच्छे गुणी गुरु और स्वामी की सीख को जो व्यक्ति सम्मान नहीं देता है, उसे भविष्य में पछताना पड़ता है और उसके जीवन में नुकसान होना निश्चित है।

## Meaning in English

Tulsidas here reiterate the importance of good Teacher/ Guru. He says that who don't listen to his teacher or guru and does not give due respect to them, is bound to regret later and face losses in life. Hence, we should always give due respect and listen to our teachers and gurus.

## Lesson For Entrepreneurs

We can get the message from this couplet is that Entrepreneur should always give due importance to their advisors/mentors and stake holders including their customers. Those entrepreneurs who do not listen to these well-wishers are bound to suffer loses. It is important to see that all well-wishers of the company are given due respect and listened carefully. They will always speak about the growth and prosperity of the organisation which is extremely necessary for the development of the business.

# 8

मुखिया मुखु सो चाहिऐ, खान पान कहुँ एक।
पालइ पोषइ सकल अंग, तुलसी सहित बिबेक।।

**भावार्थः**- तुलसीदासजी कहते हैं कि मुखिया का स्वभाव ठीक व्यक्ति के मुख के जैसा होना चाहिए जो बाहरी दृष्टिकोण से देखने में खाना-पानी स्वयं ग्रहण करता प्रतीत होता है परन्तु वो पूरे शरीर के सभी अंगो को पोषित करने का कार्य करता है।

## Meaning in English

Here Tulsidas has tried to draw a similarity between Head of Society and Mouth of the Body. Here he says that when we see a person eating or drinking, we see only the mouth doing that action for himself. But this food is nourishing the whole body and not just mouth. Similarly, the Head of the Society should also be like that. He should act in such a manner that not only he flourish but also, he should let the society also flourish along with him.

## Lesson For Entrepreneurs

Here from this couplet, we can derive that the owner should not only think of profit for himself but also distribute these profits to his employees/stake holders and consumers etc, who are also their part of business. Any wealth creation should not to be confined only to company owners but be percolated down below, to all people who has helped the company to earn those profits and wealth. The company will grow much faster and prosper more if company's all departments/ people are given some part of these profits.

# 9

सचिव बैद गुरु तीनि जौं, प्रिय बोलहिं भय आस।
राज धर्म तन तीनि कर, होइ बेगिहीं नास।।

**भावार्थः**- तुलसीदास जी कहते हैं कि मंत्री, वैद्य और गुरु ये तीनों यदि लालच वश या लाभ की लालसा में प्रिय वचन कहते हैं तो इससे राज्य, धर्म और शरीर तीनों का नाश निश्चित है।

## Meaning in English

Here Tulsidas explains if minister, doctor and teacher become greedy there will be total chaos in the society. Society will be facing Social Upheaval, Lawlessness, and loss of lives of people. There will be no control and society will see its decline and perish ultimately.

## Lesson For Entrepreneurs

Similarly, the business also works like it. If there is greediness by the owners there will be no values, integrity, and respect for doing fair business. Everyone will be only working for unethical business and profits. Such businesses practices will ultimately bring the downfall of the company as it cannot survive on unethical practices for the long run.

# 10

दया धर्म का मूल है, पाप मूल अभिमान।
तुलसी दया न छांड़िए, जब लग घट में प्राण।।

**भावार्थः**- गोस्वामीजी कहते हैं कि धर्म का मूल दया है इसलिए व्यक्ति को सदैव दया धारण करके रखनी चाहिए। पाप का मूल अभिमान में छुपा है इसलिए अभिमान का त्याग करना चाहिए और दया को धारण करना चाहिए जब तक आपका जीवन है।

## Meaning in English

Here Tulsidas says that humanity is essence of society, and it should never be forgotten. If Humanity dies Society also dies. Hence as a human being we should continue doing good and humane work till we die. It's our most important duty towards society that we keep on helping needy and poor people, whatever capacity we have. This should continue till we die.

## Lesson For Entrepreneurs

From this couplet of Tulsidas, we can derive that as the owner of a business/ company, one should always be giving something back to our employees and also back to the society.

It is the duty of entrepreneur to see that a portion of the profits are given back to needy and poor in the society without any exception. This humanly act will bring not only laurels to the company but also prosperity and growth to it, in the long run.

# 11

तुलसी इस संसार में, भांति भांति के लोग।
सबसे हस मिल बोलिए, नदी नाव संजोग।।

**भावार्थः**- तुलसीदास के दोहे में संसार को नदी मान कर अपना जीवन नाव की भांति जीने की बात कही गयी है। इस संसार में अनेक स्वभाव के लोग हैं, हमें सभी से मिल कर रहना चाहिए ठीक उसी प्रकार जिस प्रकार नाव नदी में नदी के जल से मित्रता करके तैरती हुई इस ओर से उस ओर पार हो जाती है। हम भी इस संसार रूपी सागर से आसानी से पार हो जायेंगे।

## Meaning in English

Here Tulsidas says that there are different types of people in this world. We have not only to meet them but also live with them. He connects our lives with Boat which takes different types of people from one side of river to another side. The people are different but the Boat works without being affected by the nature or types of people. Similarly, we are also in this Boat Like Life and should do our job and remain unaffected by the nature of people.

### Lesson For Entrepreneurs

We can derive from this couplet that Entrepreneur in business should act like a Boat. His company will see lots of ups and down in business cycle. During this journey entrepreneur will be meeting lots of good and bad people. But neither the company nor the entrepreneur should be bothered and influenced by these. They should just continue their good work and work towards their Goal. They will be successful ultimately.

# 12

काम क्रोध मद लोभ की, जौ लौं मन में खान।
तौ लौं पण्डित मूरखौं, तुलसी एक समान।।

**भावार्थः**- तुलसीदासजी इस दोहे में कहते हैं कि जो व्यक्ति काम, क्रोध, अहंकार, और लोभ के लिए अपना जीवन जियेगा वो कभी ज्ञान को प्राप्त नहीं कर सकता है। ऐसा व्यक्ति कोई भी हो वो मूर्ख के समान है।

## Meaning in English

Here Tulsidas says that the person who is always looking for pleasures, always angry, always arrogant, and working only for satisfying his greed. These types of persons will never get real knowledge or wisdom. These types of persons are equal to fool or ignorant person, as they are not working for knowledge but other unnecessary things and for selfish motives.

## Lesson For Entrepreneurs

From this couplet we can say that Entrepreneur should always be looking for upgradation of their product by gathering more information about, product, consumer demand and competition etc. If he is only pursuing for wealth, pleasure and is always angry and arrogant then one day everything will be lost. He will perform no better than a fool in the market. To be successful he must be aware about what is happening in the market and think about his employees and society at large.

# 13

सुख हरसहिं जड़ दुख विलखाहीं, दोउ सम धीर धरहिं मन माहीं।
धीरज धरहुं विवेक विचारी, छाड़ि सोच सकल हितकारी।।

**भावार्थः**- सुख के समय अत्यंत सुखी होना ओर दुःख में अत्यंत दुखी होना विवेकशील व्यक्ति की निशानी नहीं है। विवेकशील व्यक्ति अपने जीवन में संतुलित जीवन जीता है वो दुःख में और सुख में धैर्य के साथ-सयंम के साथ जीता है। समझदार व्यक्ति अपने जीवन में दिखावे से बचते हुए धैर्य के साथ सभी परिस्थितियों का सामना करता है।

## Meaning in English

Here Tulsidas, says that the person is not mature if he becomes extremely happy in good times and extremely sad in bad times. The person should not be worried about this cycle of times. A mature person is those who lives a balanced life. He is not very elate during good times and neither very low when time is not good. Hence, we should always live a balanced life irrespective of our times cycle.

## Lesson For Entrepreneurs

From this couplet we can derive that all businesses have

ups and downs. The Entrepreneur should not be worried when things are bad in the market and neither so happy when he is earning huge profits from market. But he should take it as a part of business life cycle and continue doing his own work. Entrepreneur should always be balanced in approach in his business and takes everything as normal in his business. Ups and downs are constant in Business.

# 14

दुर्जन दर्पण सम सदा, करि देखौ हिय गौर।
संमुख की गति और है, विमुख भए पर और।।

**भावार्थः**- दुर्जन शीशे के समान होते हैं, इस बात को ध्यान से देख लो, क्योंकि दोनों ही जब सामने होते हैं तब तो और होते हैं और जब पीछे-पीछे होते हैं तब कुछ और हो जाते हैं। भाव यह है कि दुष्ट पुरुष सामने तो मनुष्य की प्रशंसा करता है और पीठ पीछे निंदा करता है, इसी प्रकार शीशा भी जब सामने होता है तो वह मनुष्य के मुख को प्रतिबिंबित करता है; पर जब वह पीठ पीछे होता है तो प्रतिबिंबित नहीं करता।

## Meaning in English

Here Tulsidas says that a bad person is like a mirror. When you see or face mirror, it shows your image. But the moment you turn your back it changes and shows you nothing. It is same with bad person. When in front of you it will speak only good things about you. But when turn your back he will start criticising you. He will speak bad about at your back and not in front of you. Hence, we must be very careful from these types of people.

## Lesson For Entrepreneurs

From this couplet of Tulsidas we can derive that Entrepreneur should also be careful from the people who are falsely praising the company and the owners. They are always ready to put huge praises to get undue favours. But on the back of the management and owners, they are criticising the company and the owner both. They have two faces. One in front of you and another behind you. Hence Entrepreneurs and company should be avoiding these people and keep them at distance. This will help them to have less problems for themselves and for the company.

# 15

'तुलसी' काया खेत है, मनसा भयौ किसान।
पाप-पुन्य दोउ बीज हैं, बुवै सो लुनै निदान।।

**भावार्थः**- गोस्वामीजी कहते हैं कि शरीर मानो खेत है, मन मानो किसान है। जिसमें यह किसान पाप और पुण्य रूपी दो प्रकार के बीजों को बोता है। जैसे बीज बोएगा वैसे ही उसे अंत में फल काटने को मिलेंगे। भाव यह है कि यदि मनुष्य शुभ कर्म करेगा तो उसे शुभ फल मिलेंगे और यदि पाप कर्म करेगा तो उसका फल भी बुरा ही मिलेगा।

## Meaning in English

Here Tulsidas says that the body of a person is like a agriculture farm and mind is like a farmer. Good Deeds and Bad Deeds are like two Seeds. Whatever you will sow in this agricultural farm, you will get the same crop. If you sow Bad seeds crop will be bad. If you sow good seeds, you will get good crops. Hence one should do good deeds only.

## Lesson For Entrepreneurs

Here from this couplet, we can derive that every entrepreneur has an opportunity to do business in a fair and unfair way. If you choose fair means of doing business, you will always be successful and satisfied as entrepreneur. But if you choose unfair practices, you will be at the end unsuccessful and dissatisfied. Hence, as an entrepreneur he should be always be adopting honest and fair practices in his business, then only entrepreneur will be successful and happy.

# 16

अमिय गारि गारेउ गरल, नारी करि करतार।
प्रेम बैर की जननि युग, जानहिं बुध न गँवार।।

**भावार्थ**:- भगवान् ने स्त्री को अमृत और प्रेम दोनों में सानकर बनाया है। स्त्री बैर और प्रेम दोनों की जननी है, इस बात को बुद्धिमान् पुरुष जानते हैं किंतु गँवार नहीं।

## Meaning in English

Here Tulsidas says that God has created Women out of Love and Immortality. But women are not only mother of Love but can also create enmity. This fact is understood by a wise and literate man and not by a foolish and illiterate person.

## Lesson For Entrepreneurs

As an entrepreneur you should be very careful while dealing with any employees and coworkers. You must give utmost respect to women employees. All precautions should be taken for the safety and security of women coworkers. Otherwise, some undue incidence will occur with employees and can severely affect the reputation of the company resulting in huge losses to the company.

# 17

तुलसी पावस के समय, धरी कोकिलन मौन।
अब तो दादुर बोलिहं, हमें पूछिह कौन।।

**भावार्थ:**- जब बारिश का मौसम होता है तो मेढ़कों के टर्राने की आवाज इतनी तेज हो जाती है कि उसके सामने कोयल की भी आवाज कम लगने लगती है। वो अपनी ऊर्जा को व्यर्थ नहीं करता। समय अपने आप सही-गलत का एहसास करा देता है।

## Meaning in English

Tulsidas here says that when it is rainy season then numerous frogs start crocking and make lots of noise. In this time of rainy seasons Cuckoo remains silent as she understands that in the noises of frog's crocking, nobody will listen to her. Hence, she remains silent and waits for her turn after the rainy season is over.

## Lesson For Entrepreneurs

From this couplet of Tulsidas we can derive that when a businessman is surrounded by unhealthy and unfair competition, he should never adopt the corrupt practices of market but should wait for his turn. He must understand that unfair practices will not last for long and consumers will return to him and buy his product. Honest entrepreneurs should always wait patiently for right time and right place for doing business.

# 18

करम प्रधान विस्व करि राखा।
जो जस करई सो तस फलु चाखा।।

**भावार्थः**- ईश्वर ने कर्म को ही महानता दी है। उनका कहना है कि जो जैसा कर्म करता है उसको वैसा ही फल मिलता है।

## Meaning in English

Tulsidas here says that even God has put Good Deeds above everything in this world. He has given the most important thing to human beings - to do good work for the people and society at large. Every person will get the fruit of his Karma or Deeds. If person do good works, he will earn God's blessing and if he does bad deeds, he will be punished by God accordingly.

## Lesson For Entrepreneurs

Here we can derive from the couplets that an entrepreneur should not adopt corrupt and unethical practice to bring profits to the company. That will be short-lived and ultimately the company will pay for what he did. On the other hand, if he sticks and continues his honest and ethical business then one day, things will always be better and profitable for the company and its employees. Hence entrepreneur should always stick to ethical and honest way of doing business and success will ultimately come to him.

# 19

"नामु राम को कलपतरु कलि कल्यान निवासु।
जो सिमरत भयो भाँग ते तुलसी तुलसीदास।"

**भावार्थः**- राम का नाम कल्पतरु (मनचाहा पदार्थ देनेवाला) और कल्याण का निवास (मुक्ति का घर) हैं, जिसको स्मरण करने से भांग सा (निकृष्ट) तुलसीदास भी तुलसी के समान पवित्र हो गया।

## Meaning in English

Here Tulsidas says that the word Rama is like a tree which gives everything you wish. (Like a Kalpataru Tree). Rama word is also the divine way to redeem all sins and get Moksha or Divinity. He further says that by just remembering Lord Rama, a low person him (like opium plant) also become Tulsi (a divine plant). Hence, we should always remember the name of lord Rama.

## Lesson For Entrepreneurs

From this couplet we can say entrepreneurs should always follow the right and ethical path of doing business. This can only bring success to his business. Even by mistake something bad decisions have been taken, correcting with pure intention and heart will rectify it. If you are honest in your feeling and want to correct it, you will undo a bad deed with a good deed, and everything will be fine in Business.

# 20

जब काहू कै देखहिं बिपती, सुखी भए मानहुँ जग नृपति।
स्वारथ रत परिवार विरोधी, लंपट काम लोभ अति क्रोधी।

**भावार्थ:**- वे जब दूसरों को विपत्ति में देखते हैं तो इस तरह सुखी होते हैं जैसे वे ही दुनिया के राजा हों। वे अपने स्वार्थ में लीन परिवार के सभी लोगों के विरोधी, काम वासना और लोभ में लम्पट एवं अति क्रोधी होते हैं।

## Meaning in English

Here Tulsidas says, anyone who feels happy when he sees other in pain and thinks that he is the King of the World, is bound to be punished for the same. His family and his beloved ones will always be in problems and in difficulties. These people are always very greedy, running after money, always angry and never happy at all.

## Lesson For Entrepreneurs

From this couplet we can derive that any entrepreneur who feels happy when someone else business is going down, then he must remember that these bad times can come to his business also. He is not the King of the Market and one day his business will also incur losses. Hence, entrepreneur should not be greedy and running after profits; and also be compassionate when others are in trouble in business.

# 21

तुलसी देखि सुवेसु भूलहिं मूढ न चतुर नर सुंदर के किहि
पेखु बचन सुधा सम असन अहि

**भावार्थः**- सुंदर वेशभूषा देखकर मूर्ख व्यक्ति ही नहीं बुद्धिमान व्यक्ति भी धोखा खा बैठते हैं ठीक उसी प्रकार जैसे मोर देखने में बहुत ही सुंदर होता है लेकिन उसके भोजन को देखा जायें तो वह साँप और कीड़े-मकोड़े ही खाता है।

## Meaning in English

Here Tulsidas says that we should not always be impressed by appearance of a person, his clothes and wealth etc. These things may not be giving a correct picture of the person. From inside he may be different person and not so good, like he is from outside appearance. Tulsidas compared such person with Peacock which is the most beautiful bird in the world, but the food of the peacock is snakes and insects. Hence, we should always look person in totality and not just from outside appearance.

## Lesson For Entrepreneurs

From this couplet we can derive that as an entrepreneur

one should not be impressed by another businessmen's wealth and success. He may have earned this wealth by dubious manner and unethical practices. But we cannot see that what is behind his success. Hence, as an entrepreneur should always follow ethical and legal way; and not be bothered by such successful businessperson. One day the success will come to good and ethical entrepreneurs.

# 22

आगें कह मृदु वचन बनाई। पाछे अनहित मन कुटिलाई,
जाकर चित अहिगत सम भाई, अस कुमित्र परिहरेहि भलाई,

**भावार्थः**- तुलसीजी कहते हैं कि ऐसे मित्र जो कि आपके सामने बना-बनाकर मीठा बोलते हैं और मन ही मन आपके लिए बुराई का भाव रखते हैं जिसका मन साँप की चाल के समान टेढ़ा हो ऐसे खराब मित्र का त्याग कर देने में ही भलाई है।

## Meaning in English

Here Tulsidas says that we must be cautious of friends and people who speaks good in front of you but speaks negative/ play dirty game behind your back. These friends and people are like snakes who can bite anytime, and we should be away from such types of friends, as soon as possible.

## Lesson For Entrepreneurs

From this couplet we can say that entrepreneur will also come across people who are having lot of praises in front of you but will be criticising you behind your back. These people are back stabber and like snakes who can bite you whenever they get a chance. Hence entrepreneurs should stay away from these types of people and from unnecessary troublemakers.

# 23

अस्थि चर्म मय देह यह, ता सों ऐसी प्रीति
नेक जो होती राम से, तो काहे भव-भीत"

**भावार्थ:**- यह मेरा शरीर तो चमड़े से बना हुआ है जो कि नश्वर है फिर भी इस चमड़ी के प्रति इतना मोह, अगर मेरा ध्यान छोड़कर राम नाम में ध्यान लगाते तो आप भवसागर से पार हो जाते।

## Meaning in English

Here Tulsidas says that we are so worried about the body despite knowing that it is made of flesh and bones. It is going to die one day, and body will be burnt into ashes. But we still love it so much. Instead, if we love same way Lord Rama then we can be happier and more satisfied. If we love Lord Rama like that, we will certainly be getting Moksha or Salvation from the life cycle.

## Lesson For Entrepreneurs

From this couplet of Tulsidas we can derive the essence that an entrepreneur should not be running after wealth and money. Wealth had never remained with one person; it would come and go. We should rather focus on wellbeing and prosperity of our people and society at large. It will remain forever, and people will bless it with true good wishes which will bring money and prosperity automatically in return to the company.

# 24

सरनागत कहुँ जे तजहिं निज अनहित अनुमानि।
ते नर पावँर पापमय तिन्हहि बिलोकति हानि।।

**भावार्थः**- तुलसीदासजी कहते हैं कि जो मनुष्य अपने हित का विचार करके शरण में आये हुए का त्याग कर देता है वो क्षुद्र और पाप का भागी है।

## Meaning in English

Here Tulsidas says that any person who has come to seek your help and you refuse to do so, because it is not in your interest. Such people are to be condemned and are sinful. Hence the interest of the person who has come to seek your support and help, should be above everything else and must be helped whatever the person can do.

## Lesson For Entrepreneurs

From this couplet we can say that any entrepreneur to whom somebody approaches for help, he should never be refused and turned away. Even the help may not be in the interest of the entrepreneur, but if any genuine help is required then help should be given at all costs. If not given despite the ability to help, the person will not be considered a good entrepreneur and is a bad example.

# 25

माता-पिता गुरु स्वामि सिख, सिर धरि करहिं सुभाय।
लहेउ लाभु तिन्ह जनम कर, नतरु जनम जग जाये।।

**भावार्थः**- इस दोहे के माध्यम से तुलसीदासजी कहते हैं कि जो व्यक्ति अपने माता-पिता और गुरुओं के आदेश का पालन करता है उनका जन्म सिद्ध हो जाता है। इसके विपरीत जो लोग माता-पिता या गुरु के आदेशों का पालन नहीं करते उनका जन्म लेना व्यर्थ है।

## Meaning in English

Here Tulsidas says that the person who doesn't listen to his parents and teachers and who does not follow their instructions and advices. That person has no meaning in life and his birth is just a waste and without any purpose in this world.

## Lesson For Entrepreneurs

From this couplet we can derive that entrepreneurs should always follow the advice of their parents, teachers, and well-wishers. Entrepreneurs who look for good advice are always successful and prosperous. Those who do not listen to their best-wishers and advisors, are always in trouble and difficulty. Even in the case of entrepreneur is having good business, it is useless as it is of no one's benefit and neither it is beneficial to the society.

# 26

बिना तेज के पुरुष की अवशि अवज्ञा होय,
आगि बुझे ज्यों राख की आप छुवै सब कोय।"

**भावार्थः**- तेजहीन व्यक्ति की बात को कोई भी व्यक्ति महत्व नहीं देता है, उसकी आज्ञा का पालन कोई नहीं करता है। ठीक वैसे ही जैसे, जब राख की आग बुझ जाती है, तो उसे हर कोई छूने लगता है।

## Meaning in English

Here Tulsidas says that nobody listens to an unwise man and do not follow his advices. It is same as when fire is finished; the ashes has no meaning and everybody ignores it or don't respect it. People are afraid to touch fire but not afraid of touching ashes. People respect Fire and not Ashe.

## Lesson For Entrepreneurs

From this couplet we can say that entrepreneur should always give respect to advice by wise man. He should ignore unwise issues and advises. It is important to think who is having knowledge and wisdom and entrepreneur should listen to him. Rest to be ignored.

# 27

तुलसी जे कीरति चहहिं, पर की कीरति खोइ।
तिनके मुंह मसि लागहैं, मिटिहि न मरिहै धोइ।।

**भावार्थः**- इस दोहे में महाकवि तुलसीदासजी कहते हैं कि जो लोग दूसरों की बुराई कर खुद प्रतिष्ठा पाना चाहते हैं, वे खुद अपनी प्रतिष्ठा खो देते हैं। वहीं ऐसे व्यक्ति के मुंह पर एक दिन ऐसी कालिख पुतेगी जो कितनी भी कोशिश करे लेकिन मरते दम तक साथ नहीं छोड़ने वाली। यानि कि वह अपना यश और प्रतिष्ठा खोकर इस तरह से अपमानित होता हैं, कि कई कोशिशों के बाद भी उस सम्मान को दोबारा प्राप्त नहीं कर सकता है।

## Meaning in English

Here Tulsidas says that there are people who wants to get respect by criticising others and feel happy to show people small. However, ultimately these people lose their own respect in the society. They are so ridiculed by the society that they could never again get their respect back throughout their lives.

## Lesson For Entrepreneurs

From this couplet we can understand that entrepreneur

should never criticise or ridicule other people who are less in stature and wealth, than him. This type of behaviour will not be tolerated, and the entrepreneur will lose their respect in the society. Ultimately his company will also not be seen with respect in the market and will looses its reputation and ultimately all business. This respect once lost will never come back in entrepreneur's lifetime.

# 28

तनु गुन धन महिमा धरम, तेहि बिनु जेहि अभियान।
तुलसी जिअत बिडंबना, परिनामहु गत जान।।

**भावार्थः**- तन की सुंदरता, सद्‌गुण, धन, सम्मान और धर्म आदि के बिना भी जिन्हें अभिमान होता है, ऐसे लोगों का जीवन बेहद परेशानियों से भरा होता है, और उसका परिणाम भी बेहद बुरा होता है।

## Meaning in English

Here Tulsidas says that those people who don't look good, nor have good qualities, nor wealth, nor respect and nor Dharma: but still these people have lots of arrogance and attitude. These types of people live a very difficult life, and their end is also very sad and full of sorrows.

## Lesson For Entrepreneurs

From this couplet we can derive that entrepreneur who does not have good knowledge, his own self-created wealth, nor wisdom, nor earned respect in society etc and if they are still arrogant then their business life will be very difficult. They are not liked by the people and their employees and other well-wishers: and slowly the downfall of the company starts. One day the company will close and ultimately, it's an unfortunate end of the entrepreneur with no respect and love from the society.

# 29

मार खोज लै सौंह करि, करि मत लाज न ग्रास।
मुए नीच ते मीच बिनु, जे इन के बिस्वास।।

**भावार्थः**- निबुर्द्धि मनुष्य ही कपटियों और ढोंगियों का शिकार होते हैं। ऐसे कपटी लोग शपथ लेकर दोस्त बनते हैं और फिर मौका मिलते ही हमला करते हैं। ऐसे लोगों को न भगवान का भय होता है और न ही समाज का भय होता है, अर्थात ऐसे लोगों से बचना चाहिए।

## Meaning in English

Here Tulsidas says a foolish person can easily be cheated by scruples and cunning person. These people will first become friend and then will attack him whenever they get the first opportunity. These people neither have any fear of God nor fear of Society. Hence, we must be very careful from these types of people.

## Lesson For Entrepreneurs

From this couplet we can derive that Entrepreneur has to be a very intelligent and cautious person. There will be people around him who are very cunning and wants to take advantage of the ignorance of the entrepreneur. These cunning people have no respect and fear of God and of society. They will cheat whenever they get the opportunity. Hence the entrepreneur should always keep safe distance from these types of people.

# 30

जिन्ह के अति मति सहज न आई। ते सठ कत हठि करत मिताई।
कुपथ निवारि सुपंथ चलावा। गुन प्रगटै अबगुनन्हि दुरावा।

**भावार्थः**- जिनके स्वभाव में इस प्रकार की बुद्धि न हो वे मूर्ख केवल हठ करके किसी से मित्रता करते हैं। सच्चा मित्र गलत रास्ते पर जाने से रोक कर अच्छे रास्ते पर चलाते हैं और अवगुण छिपाकर केवल गुणों को प्रकट करते हैं।

## Meaning in English

Here Tulsidas says that those who have no common sense they make friends, without thinking and on their feelings and emotions. These friends are usually not true friends. However, a good friend will always keep him from doing wrong things and put him on right path. He will not show his weaknesses to the world and society at large but will only be showing good things about his friend.

## Lesson For Entrepreneurs

From this couplet we can derive that entrepreneurs should always make friends and acquaintances with great care and thought process. He must not make any instinct decision to make friends as it will not be good for his business and company. Only good friends and acquaintance will give right advice and direct the entrepreneur and company to the right path. Entrepreneur will also be benefited by good friends as they will guide the entrepreneur and the company in right perspective and manner.

# 31

देत लेत मन संक न धरई। बल अनुमान सदा हित करई।
विपति काल कर सतगुन नेहा। श्रुति कह संत मित्र गुन एह।

**भावार्थः**- मित्र लेन देन करने में शंका न करे। अपनी शक्ति अनुसार सदा मित्र की भलाई करे। वेदों के मुताबिक संकट के समय वह सौ गुणा ज्यादा स्नेह प्रेम करता है। अच्छे मित्र का यही गुण है।

## Meaning in English

Here Tulsidas says that between friends there should not be any doubt when dealing in financial matters. One should always help your friend according to your capacity and capability. A friend is loved by the person who when in need of money, is helped by his friend. A true friend quality is to help his friend when in need.

## Lesson For Entrepreneurs

From this couplet we can derive that sometime your business partner or your friend may be in financial need and requirement. Never refuse to help them if you are ina position to help them. A financial help will always be remembered by that person. You will become more closer during this crisis and when you're helping him out. He will become your true acquaintance and will also help you when in need. These are called true friends or colleagues or partners.

# 32

लखन कहेउ हँसि सुनहु मुनि क्रोध पाप कर मूल।
जेहि बस जन अनुचित करहिं चरहिं विस्व प्रतिकूल।

**भावार्थ:**- क्रोध सभी पापों की जड़ है, क्रोध में मनुष्य सभी अनुचित काम कर लेते हैं और संसार में सबका अहित ही करते हैं।

## Meaning in English

Here Tulsidas says that Anger is main cause of a person committing sins in this life. In anger person always do things which are not ethical and justified. Anger has always brought destruction in this world and must be avoided at all costs.

## Lesson For Entrepreneurs

From this couplet we can say that whenever entrepreneur takes a decision in anger, the decision will always go against him and his company and bring adverse results in the long run. Entrepreneur should always avoid taking decision in anger and wait for some time till anger is gone. Taking decision in right mind framework will always help the entrepreneur and the company.

# 33

रिपु तेजसी अकेल अपि लघु करि गनिअ न ताहु।
अजहु देत दुख रवि ससिहि सिर अवसेशित राहु।

**भावार्थः**- बुद्धिमान शत्रु के अकेले रहने पर भी उसे छोटा नही मानना चाहिए, राहु का केवल सिर बच गया था परन्तु वह आज तक सूर्य एवं चन्द्रमा को ग्रसित कर दुख देता है।

## Meaning in English

Here Tulsidas says that even if the enemy is small, he may not be taken lightly. It can be very painful like Rahu Planet. Even if Rahu's head was chopped off still, he is always creating problems for planet Sun and Moon (as per Indian Astronomical Sciences).

## Lesson For Entrepreneurs

From this couplet we can derive that while in business Entrepreneur should never overlook small problems. Even a small problem, if remains unattended can become big problem in future. These small things can keep on creating problems in the business. Hence always solve the problem; however big or small, at the very outset.

# 34

भरद्वाज सुनु जाहि जब होइ विधाता वाम।
धूरि मेरूसम जनक जम ताहि ब्यालसम दाम।।

**भावार्थ:**- महाकवि तुलसीदासजी ने यह कहा है कि- जब ईश्वर विपरीत हो जाते हैं तब उसके लिये धूल पर्वत के समान, पिता काल के समान और रस्सी सांप के समान हो जाती है।

## Meaning in English

Here Tulsidas says when God is not supporting you then Dust seems like Mountain, Father looks like Death and Ropes looks like Snake. Hence, we should always be looking for God's blessings and support.

## Lesson For Entrepreneurs

From this couplet we can derive that when things are against you in business, small problems look like mountains. Every step you take to solve the problem will be faced by many hurdles and nothing will be coming out of your efforts. Hence, we must always be looking forward to God's Blessings, good wishes of people and our good deeds/ work. If we follow this, we will overcome any hurdle we face in our business or life.

# 35

सुख संपति सुत सेन सहाई। जय प्रताप बल बुद्धि बडाई।
नित नूतन सब बाढत जाई। जिमि प्रति लाभ लोभ अधिकाई।

**भावार्थः**- सुख धन संपत्ति संतान सेना मददगार विजय प्रताप बुद्धि शक्ति और प्रशंसा जैसे-जैसे नित्य बढते हैं- वैसे-वैसे प्रत्येक लाभ पर लोभ बढ़ता है।

## Meaning in English

Here Tulsidas says that as we start getting comfort, money, property, children, army, victory, fame, intelligence, power and praises: we start to become greedy and try to have more and more of everything. This must be avoided at all costs.

## Lesson For Entrepreneurs

From this couplet we can derive that when an entrepreneur start becoming successful; his greed for wealth also becomes more and more. He starts craving for more wealth, property, fame, money, power, and profits. This greed has no limits and will continue endlessly. Hence as an entrepreneur we should be very balanced and justified for achieving success with right means and right intensions.

# 36

को न कुसंगति पाइ नसाई।
रहइ न नीच मतें चतुराई।

**भावार्थ:**- खराब संगति से सब बर्बाद हो जाते हैं। नीच लोगों के विचार के अनुसार चलने से चतुर बुद्धि भी भ्रष्ट हो जाती है।

## Meaning in English

Here Tulsidas says that if we accompany bad people then everything will be destroyed. When we live and stay with bad people, even good mind is polluted and destroyed of intelligence and right mindfulness.

## Lesson For Entrepreneurs

From this couplet we can derive that Entrepreneur should not be influenced by bad/unethical advises in business. These people will show you how to get money, profits etc through short cuts, but never listen to them. If you listen to them then your own path will be lost, and you will become dependent on them and their bad advises. Hence always avoid these kinds of people who had bad influence on you and your business. Only then you can save your company and business.

# 37

तुलसी नर का क्या बड़ा, समय बड़ा बलवान।
भीलां लूटी गोपियाँ, वही अर्जुन वही बाण।।

**भावार्थः**- गोस्वामी तुलसीदासजी कहते हैं, समय बड़ा बलवान होता है, वो समय ही है जो व्यक्ति को छोटा या बड़ा बनाता है। जैसे एक बार जब महान धनुर्धर अर्जुन का समय खराब हुआ तो वह भीलों के हमले से गोपियों की रक्षा नहीं कर पाए।

## Meaning in English

Here Tulsidas says it is the Time that is most powerful. It's the Time which makes a person big or small; and we should always respect it. Tulsidas mentioned that when time was not good, even an excellent archer like Arjun, could not protect his female followers, from Bheel community, who just attacked them with simple bow and arrows. Hence, Time is most powerful.

## Lesson For Entrepreneurs

From this couplet we can derive that Entrepreneur should never been disheartened by bad times in business. In every business there are cycles of good and bad business. If times are bad even the best efforts will not bring the desired results. On the other hand, when times are good even a small effort will be a big success. Hence as an Entrepreneur he should always be working towards the goal and keep his focus on the end results. Good Times and Bad Times will come and go, but entrepreneurs should never be affected by it.

# 38

बचन बेष क्या जानिए, मनमलीन नर नारि।
सूपनखा मृग पूतना, दस मुख प्रमुख विचारि।।

**भावार्थः**- वाणी की मधुरता और वस्त्रों की सुन्दरता से किसी भी पुरुष अथवा नारी के मन के विचारों को जाना नहीं जा सकता। क्योंकि मन से मैले शूर्पणखा, मरीचि, पूतना और दस सर वाले रावण के वस्त्र सुन्दर थे।

## Meaning in English

Here Tulsidas says that with the beautiful words and beautiful clothes one cannot understand the men or women from inside. He elaborates that character like Soopnakha, Marich, Pootna and Ravan - all has most beautiful clothes, but their Deeds were low and deplorable.

## Lesson For Entrepreneurs

Here from this couplet, we can derive that entrepreneur should not be impressed by success of other entrepreneurs as he may be successful by adopting unethical means. There are many successful businessmen who are having big businesses. But we should not be overwhelmed by their success but should be more analytical to see the reasons of his success and means he adopted.

# 39

जे न मित्र दुख होहिं दुखारी। तिन्हहि विलोकत पातक भारी।
निज दुख गिरि सम रज करि जाना। मित्रक दुख रज मेरू समाना।।

**भावार्थः**-जो मित्र के दुख से दुखी नहीं होते उन्हें देखने से भी भारी पाप लगता है।

अपने पहाड़ समान दुख को धूल के बराबर और मित्र के साधारण धूल समान दुख को सुमेरू पर्वत के समान जानना चाहिये।

## Meaning in English

Here Tulsidas says that those people who are not sad when they see their friends in trouble, are committing great sin. Even seeing these people is also a sin. One should look their own mountainous problem like dirt and see on other hand, small problem of your friend as a mountainous problem. We should always treat our friends' problems as most urgent to be solved.

## Lesson For Entrepreneurs

From this couplet we should understand that entrepreneur should never ignore the smallest problem of his employees, friend, colleagues, and well-wishers. He must take all his means to solve those problems. He must give more importance to their problems rather than his own.

# 40

देत लेत मन संक न धरई। बल अनुमान सदा हित करई।
विपति काल कर सतगुन नेहा। श्रुति कह संत मित्र गुन एहा।।

**भावार्थः**- मित्र लेन-देन करने में शंका न करे। अपनी शक्ति अनुसार सदा मित्र की भलाई करे।

वेद के मुताबिक संकट के समय वह सौ गुणा स्नेह प्रेम करता है। अच्छे मित्र का यही गुण है।

## Meaning in English

Here Tulsidas says that when your friend is in need you should always help him with all your means. The friend whom you have helped will always be hundred times more helpful and will shower love on you. Helping your friend is the True Friend's Nature.

## Lesson For Entrepreneurs

From this couplet we can derive that whenever Entrepreneur sees any of his friends, colleagues, employees, or well-wisher's in trouble; he must help them with his all means. There should not be any doubt helping them. Those whom you help in bad times will always help hundred times more than what you have done. Helping your friend is called true friendship.

# 41

सेवक सठ नृप कृपन कुमारी। कपटी मित्र सूल सम चारी।
सखा सोच त्यागहुँ मोरें। सब बिधि घटब काज मैं तोरे।

**भावार्थः**- मूर्ख सेवक, कंजूस राजा, कुलटा स्त्री एवं कपटी मित्र सब शूल समान कष्ट देने बाले होते हैं।

मित्र पर सब चिन्ता छोड़ देने पर भी वह सब प्रकार से काम आते हैं।

## Meaning in English

Here Tulsidas says that foolish servant, Miser King, Characterless Lady, and Cunning Friend – all give pain to you. Only when you give all your worries to your true friend, you are relaxed and know that your work will be done.

## Lesson For Entrepreneurs

From this couplet we can derive that an entrepreneur should always be cautious of engaging with foolish employees, cunning advisors, and characterless employees in his life. As the head of the organisation, he must take prudent decision where to spend and where not to spend company money. He must be intelligent enough to have good advisors who can give right advise to him and he can also trust them for the growth of the organisation.

# 42

सत्रु मित्र सुख दुख जग माहीं। माया कृत परमारथ नाहीं।

**भावार्थ:-** इस संसार में सभी शत्रु और मित्र तथा सुख और दुख माया झूठे हैं और वस्तुत: वे सब बिलकुल नहीं हैं।

## Meaning in English

Here Tulsidas says that in this world all enemies, friends, happiness, and sorrows are false and temporary. He says that these are all illusions and one day they will all disappear. We must not rely much on them as they are temporary and not permanent.

## Lesson For Entrepreneurs

From this couplet we as an entrepreneur should interpret that nothing is permanent in business. There will be ups and downs in business. People will come and go in the organisation. Competitors and adversaries will give you tough times. But ultimately only those will survive who are not affected by all these events. Hence an entrepreneur should always continue doing right business in righteous way. Success will come to you one day.

# 43

सुर नर मुनि सब कै यह रीती।
स्वारथ लागि करहिं सब प्रीती।

**भावार्थः**- देवता, आदमी, मुनि सबकी यही रीति है कि सब अपने स्वार्थपूर्ति हेतु ही प्रेम करते हैं।

## Meaning in English

Here Tulsidas says that God, Human Being and Saint all have common thing. They love because of some of their own need and expectation.

## Lesson For Entrepreneurs

From this couplet Entrepreneur can derive that all human beings are selfish. Either they are with you for salary, post, work given to him, or just he is knowing you personally. There must be something in you which is attracting him to join your company. Hence, we should always be understanding that everyone is here in your company for some reasons or the other. Hence entrepreneur should always be aware of these need in your people and deal accordingly. He must not be attached with anything which he come across during his business.

# 44

"गोंड़ गँवार नृपाल कलि, यवन महा महिपाल।
साम न दाम न भेद, कलि, केवल दंड कराल।।"

**भावार्थः**- तुलसीदासजी ने अपने युग की राजनीतिक विश्रृंखलता को गहराई से अनुभव किया था। उन्होंने महसूस किया कि राजा संकीर्ण विचारधारा से युक्त और आत्मकेंद्रित होते जा रहे है। प्रजा के कल्याण की ओर उनका तनिक भी ध्यान नहीं रहता है तो प्रजा के साथ-साथ उसे भी दण्ड मिलता है।

## Meaning in English

Here Tulsidas says that if the King is self-centred and always looking for his own interest then not only his people will suffer but one day King will also suffer by losing his kingdom.

## Lesson For Entrepreneurs

From this couplet we can say that if the Entrepreneur is not competent then not only his business will collapse but also his employees will also suffer. One day the company will close, and its employees will have to seek for other employment. Hence it is important for entrepreneur to be intelligent, aware, and able to survive and grow in the market.

# 45

जासु राज प्रिय राजा दुखारी।
सो नृप अवसि नरक अधिकारी।

**भावार्थः**- तुलसी ने यहाँ तक कहा कि जिस राजा के राज्य में प्रजा दुखी होती है वह राजा निश्चित रूप से नरक का अधिकारी होता है-

## Meaning in English

Here Tulsidas says if the people of a kingdom are not happy then the King will certainly go to hell. Hence the King should always look after his people and ensure their wellbeing.

## Lesson For Entrepreneurs

From this couplet we can derive that if the employees and other stakeholders are not happy with the owner or the company, then it is of no use, even if the company and owner are making huge profits. Such entrepreneurs will always be criticised and looked down on in society and one day entrepreneur will ultimately pay for all this. It is the duty of the owner to see that his employees and other stakeholders are happy and satisfied.

# 46

तुलसी किएं कुसंग थिति, होहि दाहिने बाम।
कहि सुनि सुकुचिअ सूम खल, रत हरि संकर नाम।।

**भावार्थः**- बुरी संगत में रहने से लोग बदनाम ही होते है और वो अपनी इज्जत खो देते है, जैसे देवी-देवताओं का नाम रखकर बुरी संगत में रहे तो उन पावन नामों का कोई असर नहीं होता।

## Meaning in English

Here Tulsidas says if you keep bad company then you will also become unpopular in society. It is like that even if a person keeps the name of god or goddess but, keeps bad company and have bad friends, then even his name will not be of any use.

## Lesson For Entrepreneurs

From this couplet we can derive that despite your good intention, if you have bad company, you will never be respected by the society. They will always judge you with people with whom you are acquaintance with. It is best to avoid these types of friends, employees, and other acquaintance. It will bring only problem and defame to you and your company.

# 47

करहिं जोग जोगी जेहि लागी, कोहु मोहु ममता मदु त्यागी।
व्यापकु ब्रह्मु अलखु अविनासी, चिदानंदु निरगुन गुनरासी।

**भावार्थः**- जब योगी अपने प्रभु के लिए क्रोध, मोह, ममता और अहंकार का त्याग कर देता है। वो सर्वव्यापक ब्रह्म अव्यक्त अविनासी चिदानंद निर्गुण और गुणों की खान बन जाता है।

## Meaning in English

Here Tulsidas says that when a person leaves anger, greed, affection, and arrogance, then he becomes Great Pious Soul and becomes a treasure of good deeds and become a role model for others.

## Lesson For Entrepreneurs

Here from this couplet, we can derive that as an entrepreneur you wanted to be respected in the society then you must leave all self-centred and personal goals. You must work only for your company, your people and society at large. Then people will like you to be their role model and will follow you.

# 48

कठिन कुसंग कुपंथ कराला, तिन्ह के वचन बाघ हरि ब्याला।
गृह कारज नाना जंजाला, ते अति दुर्गम सैल विसाला।

**भावार्थ:**- खराब संगत में रहना बहुत ही बुरा रास्ता है, कुसंगियों के बोल बाघ, सिंह और सांप जैसे हैं। घर के कामकाज के अनेक झंझट ही एक विशाल पहाड़ की तरह हैं।

## Meaning in English

Here Tulsidas says that if you are with wrong people then it is same as living with Lion, Tiger, and Snake. All are dangerous and must be avoided at all costs.

## Lesson For Entrepreneurs

From this couplet we can derive that as an entrepreneur you should be very careful and cautious while making friends and acquaintances. You will always be judged by people you move around. These people will always give you bad advice and benefit out of you. One day they will be the main causes of your losses and eventually the closure of your company.

# 49

सुभ अरू असुभ सलिल सब बहई, सुरसरि कोउ अपुनीत न कहई।
समरथ कहुँ नहि दोश् गोसाई, रवि पावक सुरसरि की नाई।

**भावार्थः**- गंगा में शुद्ध और अशुद्ध दोनों प्रकार का जल बहता है पर कोई उसे अपवित्र नहीं कहता। सूरज, आग और गंगा की तरह समर्थ इंसान को कोई दोष नहीं लगाता।

## Meaning in English

Here Tulsidas says that in river Ganga there is both pure and polluted water, but everyone believe that Ganga is pure and pious. Similarly, like Sun, Fire and River Ganga, no body blames a competent and able person, if he unknowingly does something wrong. They still believe in him and think it was not done intentionally.

## Lesson For Entrepreneurs

An entrepreneur should always be taking right and legal form of business and despite all problems and challenges. He should never leave the righteous path. Even some time unknowingly and unintentionally somethings go wrong, then people will never blame him for the fault. They will always stand with the entrepreneur in difficult times.

# 50

बडे सनेह लघुन्ह पर करहीं, गिरि निज सिरनि सदा तृन धरहीं।
जलधि अगाध मौलि बह फेन, संतत धरनि धरत सिर रेनू।

**भावार्थः**- बड़े हमेशा छोटों से प्रेम करते हैं। पहाड़ के सर पर हमेशा घास रहती है, समुद्र में फैन जमा रहता है और धरती के ऊपर हमेशा धूल रहती है।

## Meaning in English

Here Tulsidas says that one should always take care of small and needy people. Like there is always grass on tip of the mountain, on the surface of Ocean there is smog, and on earth surface there is dust. But all these things never have an effect on mountain, ocean or earth, similarly big people always take extreme care of people who are smaller than them and need some help.

## Lesson For Entrepreneurs

From this couplet we can derive that Entrepreneur should never forget the wellbeing of his employees and people who are under him. When a company becomes big;

the profits should also be shared with these people, who stood with the company in good and bad time. We as an entrepreneur should take utmost care of these employees and other stake holders.